BLOOMING LATE
EASY READER ONE

by

Elizabeth Grünbaum

Illustrations
by
Helga Nocker

Cover - Bouquet (section) by Johan Laurentz Jensen

Also available:

Blooming Late	—	Course Book I + CDs
Blooming Late	—	Teacher's book
Blooming Well	—	Course Book II + CDs
Blooming Well	—	Teacher's Book
Blooming Now	—	Course Book III + CDs
Blooming Now	—	Teacher's Book
Blooming Over	—	Sigrid goes to America

Easy Reader Two
Easy Reader Three -- Tosca

5.Auflage 2011 (Nachdruck)

Druck: Holzer-Druck & Medien, Weiler im Allgäu

Illustrationen: Helga Nocker
Umschlag -- Das Bouquet (Ausschnitt)
von Johan Laurentz Jensen
Design, Graphik, Layout: Grünbaum Verlag

Vertrieb: Grünbaum Verlag
Keltenring 7A
87674 Ruderatshofen
Tel.: (08343) 1060 Fax.: (08343) 585

EAN/ISBN 978-3-931006-09-9

Contents

To the Reader

In June 1994, when my "Blooming Now" students said goodbye, we were all very sad. After three years we were good friends. We said that we must keep in touch. We arranged to meet on the last Wednesday of every month. One of the students found a no-smoking café in the town. The owner said that she could organise the tables so that 16 students could sit together. In August two of our ladies were very ill. This was a terrible shock. When we had our first meeting in September, we talked about our sick friends. We all wanted to help. We wrote letters and cards — a lot of them were in English — we telephoned, we sent presents, and when they came home, we visited them. Slowly they made progress and in January they both came to the café. It was wonderful to have them back in the group.

At our meetings in the café the students often talked about their progress in English. Some were now in a normal English course in the VHS and some worked on "Blooming Late" lessons at home and practised with other students in the group. All of them said that they would like to read stories in English. They found that the English books in the book shop were too difficult. In December I wrote "A Christmas Story" for them. I took copies of it to the café.

First we talked about the new vocabulary, then I slowly read the story. The students listened carefully — and the other guests in the café listened, too! The students did the exercises at home and they discussed the themes when they practised with friends in the group. Every month I brought a new story to the café. Because the students enjoyed them so much, I decided to publish two Easy Readers for the Senioren who finish the "Blooming Late" courses. Easy Reader One has stories 1 to 4 and Easy Reader Two has stories 5 to 8.

The vocabulary and the grammar all come from the "Blooming Late" courses. However, every story has got forty to fifty new, useful words. You will find these at the end of the stories. There is also a dictionary of these new words at the back of every Easy Reader. All the other words you will find in the big dictionary at the back of "Blooming Now".

I hope that you will enjoy the stories as much as my students in Kaufbeuren.

very best wishes,
Elizabeth Grünbaum

Story 1

A Christmas Story

It was 24th December. The weather was damp, cold and windy. Everywhere looked **grey**. In the supermarket the **lights** were **bright** and Bing Crosby was singing "Jingle Bells". Mrs Clayton-Jones stood in the big queue near the **cash-desk**. In her metal shopping **basket** she had got a box of two mince pies, a very small Christmas pudding and a very small Christmas cake. She looked at her shopping. "I am not looking forward to this Christmas", she said quietly.

One year ago on Christmas Day her husband died. He was only 65 when he died. He had a **heart attack**. The ambulance came quickly to the house, but it was too late. Mrs Clayton-Jones could not believe it. Her husband was her best friend. They did everything together. Suddenly the house was empty and she was alone. When she came home after a visit to a friend or after a visit to her daughter there was no one to talk to. And now Christmas was here again — everyone had got a warm, happy house full of family and friends. Mrs Clayton-Jones did not want a Christmas tree and she did not want to decorate her house. Her daughter, a computer expert, was in America. She was there for three months. She could not come home for Christmas. "I would like to sleep through Christmas", thought Mrs Clayton-Jones.

The woman in front of Mrs Clayton-Jones had got a little child. He was probably six years old. He looked thin

The woman in front of Mrs Clayton-Jones had got a little child.

and pale. His mother looked thin and pale, too. They both wore jeans and sweaters. Their clothes looked clean but very old. In her shopping basket the woman had got a packet of bread, a box of margarine and a **bar** of chocolate. Mrs Clayton-Jones looked at her and smiled. “Your little boy is probably looking forward to Christmas Day”, she said. The woman gave a small smile. “Yes”, she said. Mrs Clayton-Jones was shocked to see big **tears** in the woman’s eyes.

“What is the matter, dear? Can I help?”, she asked. The woman shook her head. She said nothing.

“Come on,” said Mrs Clayton-Jones, “let’s **pay** for our shopping. Then I will take you to that little café next door. We will have a nice hot cup of tea and you will feel better.”

In the café the little boy smiled at his mother as the waitress **brought** him a cup of hot chocolate and a piece of iced cake. His mother smiled at him and drank some hot tea.

“Now, my dear. Tell me what is the matter. Sometimes it helps to talk about your problems”, said Mrs Clayton-Jones.

“That is kind of you,” said the woman, “but there are no **solutions** to my problems.

“Well, perhaps if you tell me, we can think of something.”

The woman was quiet for a moment.

“My husband is in **prison**”, she said. “He is from Ireland. He is really a very good man — a good husband and a good father. It was all a terrible mistake. A year ago he visited his parents in Ireland — his father was very ill. A friend, a man he knew from his childhood, asked him to bring a travelling bag back to Britain. He said OK. He had got to take it to a house near London Airport. When he arrived at the house, the police were there. They opened his bag and found two **guns** and things for making a bomb. The police **arrested** my husband and a **judge** sent him to prison for four years. As you know, Britain is very strict with Irish **terrorists**.

"But not all Irishmen are terrorists", said Mrs Clayton-Jones. "We now know that **innocent** Irishmen are in prison. You can read about this in the newspapers."

"He is innocent!", said the young woman. "He hated the **IRA**. He hated the **killing**. I told the police this, but they did not listen."

"Where do you live?", asked Mrs Clayton-Jones.

"I have got a small flat near here", said the woman. "Before my husband went to prison I worked in a good hairdressing salon. But my boss read about my husband in the newspaper and I lost my job."

"And what about Christmas?", asked Mrs Clayton-Jones.

"It will be quiet this year", said the woman and looked down.

"Can I invite you to spend Christmas in my home? It would be a great **pleasure** for me. I am alone, you see."

Mrs Clayton-Jones walked quickly back to the shopping centre. She bought some red candles, some nice pieces of holly and mistletoe and a Christmas **wreath** for her **front door.** Then she bought a small turkey, some Brussels sprouts, some young carrots, some cranberries and a bottle of rum to make rum sauce. For the little boy she bought sweets, chocolate, mandarin oranges, nuts and some small presents to put in a Christmas stocking. Then she went into the toy shop. She found the assistant.

"Could you help me, please? I would like some books and

Suddenly Mrs Clayton-Jones realised that she was happy.

toys for a little boy of six", she said.
"I am sure that we can find something for you", said the assistant and walked to the children's book department. Mrs Clayton-Jones followed. Suddenly she **realised** that she was happy.
"I am looking forward to Christmas", she said and smiled.

Mrs Clayton-Jones celebrated Christmas Day.

Vocabulary for Story 1 A Christmas Story

arrest (to) verhaften
bar (hier) Tafel
basket Korb
bright hell
bring / **brought** (to) bringen / brachte
cash desk Kasse
front door Haustür
grey grau
gun Schußwaffe
heart attack Herzinfarkt
innocent unschuldig
IRA Irish Republican Army
judge Richter
killing Töten
lights Lichter / Beleuchtung
pay / **paid** (to) zahlen / zahlte
pleasure Freude
prison Gefängnis
realise (to) begreifen / erkennen
solution Lösung
tears Tränen
terrorist Terrorist
wreath Kranz

Exercises to Story 1 - A Christmas Story

A -- Understanding the text — Please answer in complete sentences.

1) Why was Mrs Clayton-Jones not looking forward to Christmas Day?
2) Who was standing in front of Mrs Clayton-Jones in the queue ?
3) What did the little boy eat and drink in the café?
4) When did the young woman's husband visit Ireland?

5) Where did the young woman and her son live?
6) How did Mrs Clayton-Jones feel when she was in the toy shop?

B -- Puzzle — You will find all the missing words in the Vocabulary List to A Christmas Story

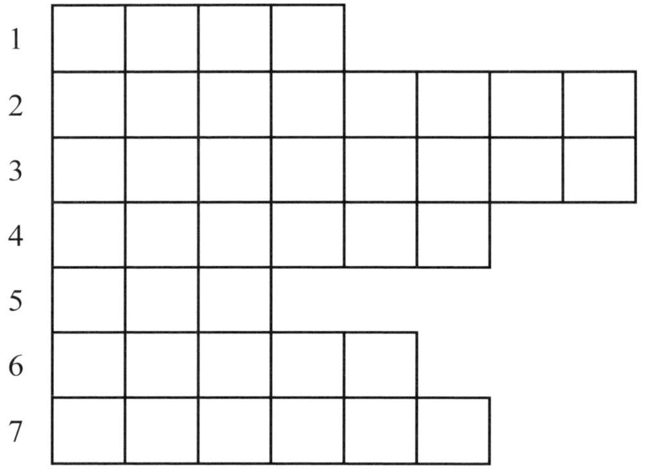

1) The opposite of lived.
2) You must pay here.
3) If you have got a problem, you need a ...
4) You carry things in this.
5) This can be very dangerous.
6) She had got ... in her eyes.
7) You decorate your house with this at Christmas.

C — Vocabulary Practice — Please complete these sentences with the correct word from the box.

1) A judge can send you to ...
2) I did not steal the ring, I am ...
3) At a bus stop, you must stand in a ...
4) I am reading my new book with great ...
5) If you read in bed, the light must be ...
6) The police always follow someone, before they ... him.

QUEUE / ARREST / PRISON INNOCENT / PLEASURE / BRIGHT

D — Discussion — Directions: If you have a friend who did the Blooming Late courses, too, perhaps you can read A Christmas Story together. Then you can talk about these topics (Themen). Remember, it is better to keep your sentences very short and simple.

1) Mrs Clayton-Jones was very sad and lonely after her husband died. What can widows do so that they are not so sad and lonely?
2) If your husband was in prison and he was innocent, what would you do?

3) Do you give presents at Christmas? What do you think about giving presents?
4) How do you usually spend Christmas Eve and Christmas Day?

You will find the answers to the exercises on pages 48-50.

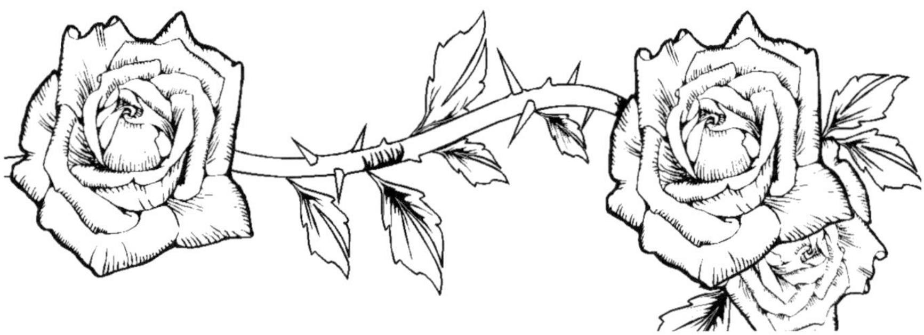

Story 2

A Summer Holiday

When we met her, Sally was young, beautiful and rich. She drove a new red Cadillac every year. She was also a widow. Her husband, a very **successful** businessman, died in a plane accident. Sally's two teenage children attended a private boarding school in Sacramento, where my husband **taught** in 1966. Soon we were good friends with her. She invited us to her large **country house** in the mountains and she invited us to her elegant **mansion** in San Francisco. Later, after my husband left the school, we often stayed with Sally in San Francisco for a weekend. The English **housekeeper** cooked marvellous meals and Sally was a **relaxed**, **charming** hostess. The guests sat around the big dinner-table and talked and laughed until the early hours of the morning. My husband and I loved our visits to Sally.

On one of those evenings in 1970 we told Sally about our summer holiday **plans**. My husband's long university **studies** were finally finished. The holiday was to be our **delayed** honeymoon. We wanted to visit family and friends in England, France, **Switzerland**, Greece and **Cyprus**, my husband's **homeland**.

"Can I come, too?" asked Sally.

"Yes, of course!" said my husband.

At that time we had not got a lot of money. My husband was still a student and I taught in a private school. Sally's husband **left** her hundreds of **valuable** IBM **shares**. She liked big hotels, she liked expensive meals, she liked elegant boutiques, she liked sleeping until midday and she liked travelling in her red Cadillac or by taxi.

"Oh dear!" I thought. "There will be problems with Sally."

"Never mind," said my husband as we **packed** our suitcases. "She is a very good friend. We must **do our best**."

We visited England alone and then we met Sally in Paris. Sally stayed in a big expensive hotel near the Champs Elysées. We stayed in a little hotel in Montmartre. But that was all right. We travelled by underground to her hotel and met her at midday.

The first big problem, however, came at dinner. My husband **translated** the **menu** for Sally. Then she chose a **dish**.

"Can you ask the waiter, if there are green peppers in it? I am terribly **allergic** to green peppers." she said.

"Yes, there are, Sir." **answered** the waiter.

So Sally asked about another dish — and another — and another — and another ... This happened in every restaurant for the next three weeks and my husband is not a very **patient** man!

The second big problem came on the next day. Sally had never got enough money in her **purse**. She did not understand the **foreign** money. So she asked my husband to pay for her.

"You will make a **list**. I will **pay** you **back** every three days." she said.

My husband paid for all Sally's meals, taxis, **entrance tickets**, shopping, cups of coffee and glasses of lemonade. Every three days he gave the list to Sally. She looked at it very **suspiciously**.

"Did I spend all that?" she always asked and she looked at the list for a long time before she paid.

My husband translated the menu for Sally.

My husband felt **uncomfortable**. He was angry with Sally. However, he did not say anything.
We **survived** Paris, Zürich and Athens. The third big problem came on the plane to Cyprus. Sally ate green peppers. She suddenly felt very, very hot and she **vomited**. She looked terrible!
We **planned** to travel by bus in Cyprus. Because of Sally's illness, we had got to rent a car at the airport. My husband rented a small, grey British **sports car** and we drove to our holiday flat in Nicosia. Sally looked very pale and very weak. My husband telephoned an old friend. The friend said that there was a good **clinic** near the President's Palace. At that time Archbishop Makarios was the President of Cyprus.
Nicosia is a difficult city full of old, narrow streets. My husband could not find the clinic. Finally, he stopped and asked a man at a **petrol station**.
"Where is the President's Palace, please?" he asked. The man showed him the way.
In the clinic Sally went to bed in a quiet room and the doctor gave her an **injection**. My husband and I went to a restaurant and ate a small meal. Then we drove back to our holiday flat. It was now midnight. The streets were **cool** and dark. As we parked our car, a man walked out of the **shadows**. He spoke to my husband in Greek. I looked around me and saw a group of four **dark-skinned** men. One man was cleaning his **finger nails** with a long, **sharp** knife. The other men were looking at us. I felt a cold hand inside my stomach and my **blood** changed to **ice**. "This is a **street gang**", I thought, "They want to **kill** us."
I looked in panic at my husband. He was still speaking Greek with the man from the shadows. Suddenly, they both shook

One man was cleaning his finger nails with a long knife.

hands and said goodbye.
“Come on,” my husband said to me and we **walked past** the group of dark-skinned men and up the stairs into our holiday flat. My husband closed the door and I sat down. I was **trembling** and I could not speak for a few seconds. Finally, I said, “What was the matter?“
My husband **yawned** and began to **take off** his clothes.
“It was very **funny**, actually.” he said. “That man was from the police **headquarters**. Apparently, six months ago a man and two women tried to kill President Makarios. They drove a small, grey British sports car. That man we talked to at the petrol station thought we were those people again! He went at once to the police and gave them our **car number**. The police found us easily. But don’t worry! Everything is OK. The detective knows that we are quite **harmless**!”
“And what about the dark-skinned men outside the flat?” I asked.
“Those men”, said my husband as he cleaned his teeth, “are our neighbours. They knew that the man was from the police headquarters. Island people are always very **curious**.”
Next morning the men were outside again. They sat on chairs in the sunshine and they **waved** and smiled as we walked to our car. In the clinic Sally was **fit and well** again.

“**Gee, you guys**”, she said. “Thanks for everything yesterday. Now — how much money do I **owe** you?”
My husband **groaned** quietly.

Vocabulary for Story 2 A Summer Holiday

allergic to allergisch gegen
answer (to) antworten
blood Blut
car number Autokennzeichen
charming reizend
clinic Klinik
cool abgekühlt
country house Landhaus
curious neugierig
Cyprus Zypern
dark-skinned dunkelhäutig
delayed aufgeschoben
dish Gericht
do your best (to) sein Bestes tun
entrance tickets Eintrittskarten
finger nail Fingernagel
fit and well wohlauf
foreign fremd
funny (hier) komisch
Gee you guys Mensch (Meier), Kinder
groan (to) stöhnen
harmless harmlos
headquarters Zentrale
homeland Heimat
housekeeper Haushälterin
ice Eis (Würfel)
injection Spritze
kill (to) töten
leave / left (to) (hier) vererben / vererbte
list Liste
mansion Villa
menu Speisekarte
owe (to) schulden
pack (to) packen
patient geduldig
pay back (to) zurückzahlen
paid back zurückzahlte
petrol station Tankstelle
plan (to) vorhaben
plans Pläne
purse Geldbeutel
relaxed entspannt
shadow Schatten
shares Aktien
sharp scharf
sports car Sportwagen
street gang Straßenbande

studies Studium
successful erfolgreich
survive (to) überleben
suspiciously mißtrauisch
Switzerland Schweiz
take off (to) (hier) Kleider ausziehen
teach / taught (to) unterrichten/unterrichtete
translate (to) übersetzen
tremble (to) zittern
uncomfortable beklommen
valuable wertvoll
vomit (to) sich übergeben
walk past (to) vorbeigehen
wave (to) winken
yawn (to) gähnen

Exercises to Story 2 A Summer Holiday

A -- Understanding the text — Please answer in complete sentences.

1) How do we know that Sally was very rich?
2) Why did the narrator (Erzähler) think that a holiday with Sally would be difficult?
3) What was Sally's problem in restaurants?
4) When did the narrator's husband get angry with Sally?
5) Where was the good clinic in Nicosia?
6) Who waited outside the narrator's holiday flat in Nicosia at midnight?

B -- Puzzle — Find 10 verbs. You will find them all in the Vocabulary List to *A Summer Holiday*

	1	2	3	4	5	6	7	8
A	A	G	L	P	U	T	J	V
B	G	R	O	A	N	Y	K	O
C	B	H	M	P	T	Z	T	M
D	C	I	Y	A	W	N	R	I
E	S	U	R	V	I	V	E	T
F	D	J	N	Q	U	A	M	L
G	P	A	Y	R	V	G	B	M
H	E	W	A	V	E	H	L	N
I	F	K	O	S	W	I	E	O
J	K	I	L	L	X	O	W	E

C -- Vocabulary Practice — Please complete these sentences. You will find all the missing words in the Vocabulary List to *A Summer Holiday*

1) I cannot drink milk. I am ________ / ________milk.
2) If the teacher asks me a difficult question in English, I feel

____________ .
3) The policeman looked ______________at the man with the big red sports car.

4) I arrived in Munich one hour late. My plane was __________.

5) Bulls are dangerous, but cows are ______________ .

6) My mother-in-law asks a lot of questions about the children. She is very _________________.

D -- Discussion — Directions: If you have a friend who did the Blooming Late courses, too, perhaps you can read A Summer Holiday together. Then you can talk about these topics. Remember, it is better to keep your sentences very short and simple.

1) Do you like going on holiday with friends? Why?
2) Can you remember when you were very frightened? Can you talk about it?
3) Which is your favourite country when you go on holiday? Why? Is there a country you still want to visit very much?
4) Which was the best holiday you ever had?

You will find the answers to the exercises on pages 48-50.

Story 3

The Accident

Herr and Frau Weber did not know anything about dogs. When Herr Weber was a child, his parents were often frightened of dogs. Frau Weber's parents were doctors. They always said that dogs carried **germs**. Herr and Frau Weber's two little sons **begged** their parents for a dog.

"No!" said Frau Weber. "You can have a rabbit."

But the two boys were not **satisfied**. They saw a photo of a dog in the **local newspaper**. The Animal Home had got a one-year-old **wire-haired** Dachshund. It was Christmas time so Herr and Frau Weber **gave in**.

The lady in the Animal Home said that Sammy was a very lukky dog. His first owner, a lady, died in a car accident. She was returning to Germany after a holiday in South Tyrol. She drove too quickly in the mountains. Her car fell down the **mountainside**. Sammy survived the accident. Everyone said that it was a **miracle**.

Sammy soon **settled down** in his new home. He was **intelligent** and **affectionate**. The two boys loved him. He followed them up the stairs to their bedrooms on the third **floor**, and he followed them down the stairs to their **playroom** in the cellar. He **barked** loudly when someone came to the house. He wanted to **protect** his new family and his new home. Herr and Frau Weber soon loved him, too. They had got only one **complaint**. Sammy did not want to travel by car. **Every time** they carried him into the

Sammy soon settled down in his new home. The two boys loved him.

car, he trembled and cried. He **jumped out** at once. It was **clear** that he remembered the accident.
"We must be patient with him," said Frau Weber.
When summer came, Sammy's **fear** of cars was a problem. The Webers had got a holiday house near Lago Maggiore in Italy. Every summer they drove down to the house and stayed there for six weeks.
"Sammy will come, too," said the boys.
"Of course," said Frau Weber and **frowned**. Finally she talked to the **vet**. He suggested a **sedative** for Sammy. Frau Weber smiled in **relief**.
As always, the Webers packed the car the evening before they travelled. Sammy watched Frau Weber pack the suitcases. He followed Herr Weber outside to the car. He watched him **put** the suitcases into the boot. Suddenly, Sammy jumped into the car and stood on the **back seat**. He looked at Herr Weber and **wagged** his **tail**. He wanted to go on holiday with his family. His **phobia** was no longer a problem.
The Weber sons **grew up**. They went to **grammar school** and then to university. **By this time** Sammy was 12 years old. He could no longer follow the boys up and down the stairs. Like a lot of Dachshunds, he had got rheumatism in his **back legs**. He was **lame**. Every summer, however, he still went to Italy by car. He stayed inside the cool house or he lay under the big tree in the garden.
One summer afternoon the family **decided** to go for a walk in the mountains around Lago Maggiore. They drove up the narrow **road** to the **top** of the mountain and parked. Sammy jumped out and walked to the **edge** of the road. Suddenly, the

"It is incredible!" said the vet. "He has got scratches on his mouth and nose, but that is all!"

Webers heard a **noise**. **Stones** were falling. The family looked and saw Sammy disappear down the mountainside. **Horrified**, they ran to the edge and shouted, "Sammy! Sammy!" But there was only **silence**. They looked down the mountain, but they could see nothing.

Herr Weber **led** the family down the small mountain **path**. They went as quickly as they could. Sammy was lying on his back. His eyes were closed. There was blood on his mouth and his nose. His little legs were **stiff**. He was **unconscious**. The younger son **lifted** Sammy **up** carefully. The family returned to the car in silence.

"We must find a vet," said Frau Weber. They drove thirty kilometres to the nearest town, but the vet was closed. The family remembered that it was a **national holiday**.

Sadly the Webers drove back to their holiday house. The younger son sat in the **front seat** next to his father. Sammy lay in his arms. Tears ran down the young man's face. His father drove into the **driveway** of their house and parked. Herr Weber got out and opened the car door for his son. There was a small **movement**. Herr Weber could not believe what he saw. Sammy jumped out of the car and walked across the garden to his **water bowl** under the tree! He looked absolutely fit and well — and he was no longer lame! He could walk normally.

Next day Herr and Frau Weber took Sammy to the vet.

"It is incredible!" said the vet. "He has got **scratches** on his mouth and nose, but that is all! I cannot tell you why he is no longer lame. I think it was the shock of the **fall**. By the way, he cannot see with his left eye. Perhaps that is why he fell."

Sammy enjoyed four more summers at Lago Maggiore before he died very peacefully at the age of sixteen.

Vocabulary for Story 3 The Accident

affectionate liebevoll
back seat Rücksitz
back leg Hinterbein
bark (to) bellen
beg (to) betteln
by this time inzwischen
clear deutlich
complaint Beanstandung
decide (to) beschließen
driveway Auffahrt
edge Rand
every time jedes Mal
fall Sturz
fear Angst
floor Stockwerk
front seat Vordersitz
frown (to) die Stirn runzeln
germs Bazillen
give in / gave in (to) nachgeben / gab nach
grammar school Gymnasium
grow up / grew up (to) aufwachsen / wuchs auf
horrified entsetzt
intelligent intelligent
jump out (to) hinausspringen
lame lahm / gelähmt
lead / led (to) führen / führte
lift up (to) hochheben
local newspaper Lokalzeitung
miracle Wunder
mountainside Bergabhang
movement Bewegung
national holiday gesetzlicher Feiertag
noise Geräusch
path Pfad
phobia Phobie
playroom Spielzimmer
protect (to) schützen
put (to) stellen
relief Erleichterung
road Straße
satisfied zufrieden

scratch Kratzer
sedative Beruhigungsmittel
settle down (to)
sich einleben
silence Stille
stiff steif
stone Stein
tail Schwanz
top Gipfel
unconscious bewußtlos
vet Tierarzt
wag (to) wedeln
water bowl Wassernapf
wire-haired rauhaarig

Exercises to Story 3 The Accident

A/1 -- Understanding the text — Please answer in complete sentences.
1) How did the Weber sons know about Sammy?
2) Why was Sammy frightened of cars?
3) Where did the Webers always spend their summer holidays?
4) What did the Webers think when they found Sammy lying unconscious?
5) Who carried Sammy back to the car?
6) When did the Webers know that Sammy was not dead?

A/2 -- Questions on the text — Please make four questions on the text. Begin your questions with **where**, **when**, **what** and **why**. Then give answers to your questions.

B-- Puzzle — Put the answers to the questions below in the boxes. You will find all the words in the Vocabulary List to Story 3 The Accident

1										
2										
3										
4										
5										
6										

1) What a dog does with his tail
2) What a dog must not do when his owners are eating
3) The noise a dog makes
4) The opposite of front leg
5) The dish a dog drinks water from
6) A sort of Dachshund

C -- Vocabulary Practice — Please complete the sentences in Linda's letter. The words all come from Story 3 The Accident and are in the "Denkblase"

Linda

driveway
relief
lift
satisfied
decided
noise
floor
stiff
horrified
unconscious
complaint
scratches

Dear Sigrid,

I am writing this letter to you from hospital. Last week I had an accident. It happened on Monday, when I 1) __________ to clean the bedroom windows. As you know, our bedroom is on the first 2) ______. You will be 3) _____________ to hear that I fell from the window onto the 4) _________. John heard the 5) _________. He ran outside and found me 6) _________ . An ambulance took me to hospital. To my 7) ____________ I have only got a broken arm and a few 8) ___________ on my leg. My arm is getting better, but it is still 9) __________ and I still cannot 10) ___________________ it up.

I do not like hospital life. My big 11) ___________ is the food. It is very bad. Never mind. Tomorrow I can go home. John will cook a good Italian meal and I will be 12) _____________. I will telephone you next week.

Love,
Linda

D -- Discussion — Directions: If you have a friend who did the Blooming Late courses, too, perhaps you can read The Accident together. Then you can talk about these topics. Remember, it is better to keep your sentences very short and simple.

1) Did you ever have a car accident? Tell your partner about it.
2) Do you like dogs? Have you got a dog? Tell your partner about your dog or about a dog you know.
3) Why do people buy holiday homes? Do you think holiday homes are a good idea?
4) Why do people like walking in the mountains? Which safety rules should people remember when they walk in the mountains?

You will find the answers to the exercises on pages 48-50.

Story 4

School Days

I was lucky. I had a very good mother and a very good grandmother. I was my mother's first child and my grandmother's first grandchild. I was very important to them both. During the war years we lived in my grandparents' house in North Wales. My father was not there. He was in **India**, in the army. My grandparents' house was small. My mother's younger brother and sister also lived there. The house was full of people, we had not got a lot of money, but we lived together happily. My grandparents were peaceful, tolerant people. They also laughed a lot, — my grandmother had a wonderful sense of humour.

When I was a young child, my life in this family was **perfect**. Everyone loved me. Nobody ever **smacked** me. Nobody shouted at me. Nobody even **scolded** me. Until I was five I cannot remember a bad moment in my life. Then, suddenly, at the age of five I **experienced** real fear for the first time.

I was five. It was September, and like all British children I had got to go to school. The teacher in the first class of our elementary school was **notorious**. She was called Miss Edith James. She taught my mother and all my uncles and my aunts. She taught everyone in this small town in the Welsh mountains. She was an **old maid** — very small, very thin and very strict. Her **straight** grey hair was in a **tight knot** behind her head, her eyes were cold, her nose was sharp and **pointed** and she wore tiny metal

The teacher in the first class of our elementary school was notorious.

glasses. Her mouth was angry and hard. She never smiled. She wore narrow leather shoes with very tight **laces**.

My mother took me to school on the first day. All the new children looked at Miss James and cried loudly. I **clung** to my mother's coat.
"Please, don't go," I begged.
But Miss James **sent** all the mothers home.
"**Be quiet**, please — at once!" she said to us. We were all quiet at once. She gave us little paper **mats**. We had got to **weave** narrow pieces of paper into the mats. I could not do it. Every time Miss James walked past I put my hand on my mat. I hoped she could not see it. Suddenly, Miss James was very angry with two older children in the class. She shouted loudly. The children walked to her **desk**. They **held out** their hands. I **froze** in horror as she hit the children's hands with a thick, black **ruler**. My stomach was like a hard **ball**. I was now **terrified** of Miss James!

I stayed in Miss James's class for two years. I was always frightened of her, but I was good at writing and reading. She was angry with a lot of children, but she was never angry with me — until one day. It was in my second year. My best friend was called Bethan. One evening in early summer we went for a walk together. We found some beautiful red **rhododendrons** in a small **wood**. We **picked** some. Then I had an idea.
"We can go to different houses in the town and sell them," I said.
Bethan thought this was a marvellous idea. We knocked on a lot of doors, but we could not sell any rhododendrons. Finally, we knocked on Miss James's door. She opened it and looked at us coldly.

"Where did you pick those flowers?", she asked.
"In the wood," I said. Miss James closed the door.

Next day in school, Miss James began the day with the usual Bible story and **prayer**. Then she said, "Glenys and Bethan — stand in front of the class."
I was so frightened that I almost could not walk from my desk to the front of the class. I felt cold and sick. Miss James looked at the class of **silent** children. "Yesterday these two girls stole some flowers. Then they came to my house. They wanted to sell the stolen flowers. Stealing is a **crime**. The police put people who steal in prison for a long time! I should really take these two girls to the police station. I should tell the police that these girls are **thieves**! Next time I will take you to the police, Glenys and Bethan. Hold out your hands." Whack. Whack ... She hit our small hands with her thick, black ruler six times. She told us to stand in the corner. We stood in the corner all morning.

After school I walked home and went into the **bathroom**. I **locked** the door and sat on the toilet and cried **bitterly**. When I finally went into the living-room, my grandmother looked at me.
"Come and have a nice cup of tea," she said.
I drank the tea and I felt better.
"Now — What's the matter?", my grandmother asked.
I looked at my grandmother and I **hesitated**. Then I told her the story of the rhododendrons. I told her how terrified I was of Miss James. I told her everything.

"We can go to different houses in the town and sell them."

My grandmother did not speak. She stood up and went to the cupboard and took out a bottle of aspirins — she took two and finished her cup of tea. Then she went into the **hall** and put on her coat and hat — she always wore a hat — and she took her handbag. She left the house and she came back an hour later.
"Don't worry about Miss James, Glenys. Everything is all right now.", she said and she went into the kitchen to make my grandfather's supper.

Next day after prayers Miss James stood by her desk.
"There is something I want to say before we begin the arithmetic lesson.", she said. "Yesterday I was very angry with Glenys and Bethan. I made a mistake. These girls did not steal the flowers. The flowers grew on **public property.** I made a mistake. I am sorry. Now open your arithmetic books."
Bethan looked at me and I smiled — but very quickly.

I was fifteen when my grandmother told me what she said to Miss James that day.
"Well," she said, " first I told her that you did not steal the rhododendrons. Then I told her that she should not **frighten** little children with stories of police and prison. Finally, I **reminded** her of her own school days. She and I were in the same class all through school. I reminded her of the day I lost a very expensive black silk hair **ribbon** in school. It was a birthday present from my father. I had got very beautiful **chestnut curls** and I always wore a ribbon at the back. Edith James had got pale, thin, straight hair. She was always **jealous** of me. When we put our coats on to go home I looked at her satchel. It was half open and I saw my ribbon. I took it out and showed her.

"Oh please, don't tell the headmaster! Please, don't tell my father!", she begged and began to cry.
I did not tell anyone. But that day I went to her house I said, "Edith, I did not tell anyone about the black silk ribbon you stole from me in school. But if you do not **apologise** to my granddaughter and her friend in front of the class, I will tell. It is never too late, you know."
My grandmother smiled. "Do you remember? She **retired** at the end of the year."

Vocabulary for Story 4 School Days

apologise (to) sich entschuldigen
ball Ball
bathroom Badezimmer
Be quiet! Seid still!
bitterly bitterlich
chestnut (hier) kastanienfarbig
cling / **clung** (to) festklammern / klammerte fest
crime Verbrechen
curls Locken
desk Pult
experience (to) erleben
freeze / **froze** (to) erfrieren / erfror
frighten (to) erschrecken
hall Hausflur
hesitate (to) zögern
hold out / **held out** (to) hinhalten / hielt hin
India Indien
jealous eifersüchtig
knot (hier) Haarknoten
laces (hier) Schnürsenkel
lock (to) verschließen
mat Untersetzer
notorious berüchtigt
old maid alte Jungfer
perfect perfekt
pick (to) pflücken
pointed spitzig
prayer Gebet

public property öffentliches Eigentum
remind (to) jdn an etwas erinnern
retire (to) in den Ruhestand treten
rhododendrons Rhododen-dren
ribbon (Haar-) Schleife
ruler Lineal
scold (to) beschimpfen
send / sent (to) schicken / schickte
silent (hier) totenstill
smack (to) einen Klaps geben
straight (hier) glatt
terrified (to be) erschrocken sein
thief / thieves Dieb
tight (hier) fest
weave / wove (to) weben / webte
wood (hier) kleiner Wald

Exercises to Story 4 School Days

A/1 -- Understanding the text — All these sentences are wrong. Please write them correctly.

1) Glenys was terrified of her grandmother.
2) Miss James was kind and tolerant and she had got a good sense of humour.
3) The new children in Miss James's class had got to make dolls with narrow pieces of paper.
4) Miss James said that selling rhododendrons was an excellent idea.
5) Glenys and Bethan had got to stand outside the classroom all morning.
6) Glenys's grandmother apologised to Miss James.

A/2 -- Questions on the text — Please make four questions on the text. Begin your questions with **who**, **what**, **when** and **why**. Then give answers to your questions.

B -- Puzzle — Put the missing words for the text below in the boxes. You will find all the words in the Vocabulary List to Story 4 School Days

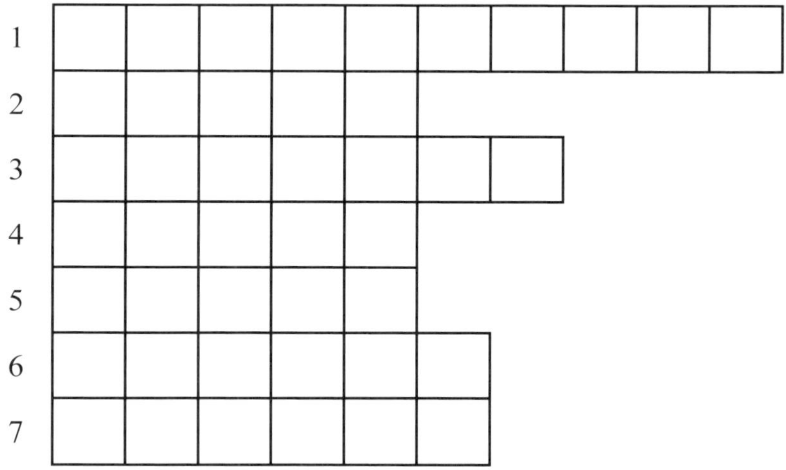

Miss James taught the first class in a school in a small Welsh town. She 1) — the children, because she was so strict and because she hit them with a 2) — . Miss James did not marry. She was an 3) —. The children cried when they saw Miss James and 4) — to their mothers' coats. Miss James had got straight grey hair which she wore in a 5) — knot. Her eyes were cold and her nose was 6) — . All the children were happy when Miss James 7) — .

C -- Vocabulary Practice — Please find the opposites of these words. You will find all the words in the Vocabulary List to Story 4 School Days

1) straight hair : ______________________
2) famous : ______________________
3) private property : ______________________
4) to work : ______________________
5) noisy : ______________________
6) imperfect : ______________________
7) to unlock : ______________________
8) a married woman : ______________________

D — Discussion — Directions: If you have a friend who did the Blooming Late courses, too, perhaps you can read School Days together. Then you can talk about these topics. Remember, it is better to keep your sentences very short and simple.

1) Did you ever have a very strict teacher? Tell your partner about the teacher or talk about a strict teacher you knew.

2) Did you live near your grandparents when you were a child? Tell your partner about them. Did you like them? Were they strict or easy-going? Had they got hobbies? What were they good at?
3) What do you think? Should teachers hit children? Should parents hit children? Why?
4) Can you remember a time when your mother was very angry with you? Tell your partner about it.

You will find the answers to the exercises on pages 48-50.

Answers to the Exercises

Story 1 A Christmas Story

A — Understanding the text —

1) She was not looking forward to Christmas Day, because her husband died one year ago at Christmas.
2) A young woman and her son were standing in front of Mrs Clayton-Jones in the queue.
3) The little boy ate a piece of iced cake and drank a cup of hot chocolate.
4) He visited Ireland one year ago.
5) They lived in a flat near the shopping centre.
6) She felt very happy.

B — Puzzle

1) died / 2) cash-desk / 3) solution / 4) basket / 5) gun / 6) tears / 7) wreath

C — Vocabulary Practice —

1) prison / 2) innocent / 3) queue / 4) pleasure / 5) bright / 6) arrest

Story 2 A Summer Holiday

A — Understanding the text —

1) We know she was very rich, because she bought a new Cadillac every year, because she had got a big country house in the mountains and an elegant mansion in San Francisco, and

because her husband left her hundreds of valuable IBM shares.
2) The narrator thought that a holiday with Sally would be difficult, because Sally liked big hotels, expensive meals, elegant boutiques, sleeping until midday and travelling in her red Cadillac or by taxi.
3) Sally was allergic to green peppers.
4) The narrator's husband got angry, when Sally did not want to pay back the money he spent for her food, drinks, taxis, etc.
5) The clinic in Nicosia was near the president's palace.
6) A detective and four dark-skinned men waited outside the holiday flat in Nicosia.

B — Puzzle
D/3) yawn / J/6 owe / A/8 vomit / A/4 put / H/2 wave / G/1 pay / B/1 groan / J/1 kill / E/1 survive / C/7 tremble

C — Vocabulary Practice —
1) allergic to / 2) uncomfortable / 3) suspiciously /
4) delayed / 5) harmless / 6) curious

Story 3 The Accident

A/1 — Understanding the text —
1) They saw his photo and they read about him in the local newspaper.
2) Sammy was frightened of cars, because his first owner had a bad car accident.
3) The spent their holidays in Italy, near Lago Maggiore.

4) They thought that Sammy was dead.
5) The younger son carried Sammy back to the car.
6) The knew that Sammy was not dead, when he jumped out of the car.

B — Puzzle
1) wag / 2) beg / 3) bark / 4) back leg / 5) water bowl / 6) wire haired

C — Vocabulary Practice —
1) decided / 2) floor / 3) horrified 4) driveway / 5) noise / 6) unconscious / 7) relief / 8) scratches / 9) stiff / 10/ lift / 11) complaint / satisfied

Story 4 School Days

A/1 — Understanding the text —
1) Glenys was not terrified of her grandmother. She was terrified of Miss James.
2) Miss James was not kind and tolerant and she had not got a good sense of humour. She was strict with the children and she frightened them.
3) The new children in Miss James's class had not got to make dolls with narrow pieces of paper. The had got to weave narrow pieces of paper into mats.
4) Miss James did not say that selling rhododendrons was an excellent idea. She said that it was a crime. She said the police could take people who steal to prison.

5) Glenys and Bethan had not got to stand outside the classroom all morning. They had got to stand in the corner all morning.
6) Glenys' grandmother did not apologise to Miss James. She reminded Miss James of the time she stole a ribbon in school. She said that Miss James had got to apologise to Glenys and Bethan.

B — Puzzle —
1) frightened / 2) ruler / 3) old maid / 4) clung / 5) tight / 6) pointed / 7) retired

C — Vocabulary Practice —
1) curls / 2) notorious / 3) public property / 4) to retire / 5) silent / 6) perfect 7) to lock / 8) an old maid

Dictionary

Hier finden Sie sämtliche Wörter des Buches in alphabetischer Reihenfolge. Neben dem englischen Stichwort und der deutschen Übersetzung sehen Sie auch, wo das betreffende englische Wort zum ersten Mal auftritt (Fundstelle). Die Nummer der Fundortangabe weist auf die Story hin, in der das Wort vorkommt. I/1 heißt also Easy Reader One, Story 1, und I/2 heißt Easy Reader One, Story 2, etc.

affectionate liebevoll I/3
allergic to allergisch gegen I/2
answer (to) antworten I/2
apologise (to)
sich entschuldigen I/4
arrest (to) verhaften I/1
back seat Rücksitz I/3
back-leg Hinterbein I/3
ball Ball I/4
bar (hier) Tafel I/1
bark (to) bellen I/3
basket Korb I/1
bathroom Badezimmer I/4
Be quiet! Seid still! I/4
beg (to) betteln I/3
bitterly bitterlich I/4
blood Blut I/2
bright hell I/1
by this time
inzwischen I/3
car number
Autokennzeichen I/2
cash desk Kasse I/1
charming reizend I/2
chestnut (hier) kastanienfarbig I/4
clear deutlich I/3
cling / clung (to)
festklammern / klammerte fest I/4
clinic Klinik I/2
complaint Beanstandung I/3
cool abgekühlt I/2
country house Landhaus I/2
crime Verbrechen I/4
curious neugierig I/2
curls Locken I/4
Cyprus Zypern I/2
dark-skinned dunkelhäutig I/2
decide (to) beschließen I/3
delayed aufgeschoben I/2
desk Pult I/4
die / died (to) sterben
starb I/1
dish Gericht I/2
do your best (to)
sein Bestes tun I/2
driveway Auffahrt I/3
edge Rand I/3
entrance tickets Eintrittskarten
I/2

every time jedes Mal I/3
experience (to) erleben I/4
fall Sturz I/3
fear Angst I/3
finger nail Fingernagel I/2
fit and well wohlauf I/2
floor Stock I/3
follow (to) folgen I/1
foreign fremd I/2
freeze / **froze** (to)
erfrieren I/4
frighten (to) erschrecken I/4
front door Haustür I/1
front-seat Vordersitz I/3
frown (to)
die Stirn runzeln I/3
funny komisch I/2
Gee, you guys Mensch
(Meier), Kinder I/2
germs Bazillen I/3
give in / **gave in** (to)
nachgeben I/3
grammar school
Gymnasium I/3
grey grau I/1
groan (to) stöhnen I/2
grow up / **grew up** (to)
aufwachsen / wuchs auf I/3
gun Schußwaffe I/1
hall Hausflur I/4
harmless harmlos I/2
headquarters Zentrale I/2
heart attack Herzinfarkt I/1
hesitate (to) zögern I/4
hold out / **held out** (to)
hinhalten I/4
homeland Heimat I/2
horrified entsetzt I/3
housekeeper Haushälterin I/2
ice Eis (Würfel) I/2
in a queue
Schlange stehen I/1
India Indien I/4
injection Spritze I/2
innocent unschuldig I/1
intelligent intelligent I/3
jealous eifersüchtig I/4
judge Richter I/1
jump out (to)
hinausspringen I/3
kill (to) töten I/2
knot (hier) Haarknoten I/4
laces (hier) Schnürsenkel I/4
lame lahm / gelähmt I/3
lead / **led** (to)
führen / führte I/3
leave / **left** (to) (hier)
vererben I/2
lift up (to) hochheben I/3
lights Lichter /Beleuchtung I/1
list Liste I/2
local newspaper
Lokalzeitung I/3
lock (to) verschließen I/4
mansion Villa I/2
mat Untersetzer I/4

menu Speisekarte I/2
miracle Wunder I/3
mountainside Bergabhang I/3
movement Bewegung I/3
national holiday
gesetzlicher Feiertag I/3
noise Geräusch I/3
notorious berüchtigt I/4
old maid alte Jungfer I/4
owe (to) schulden I/2
pack (to) packen I/2
path Pfad I/3
patient geduldig I/2
pay / **paid** (to)
zahlen / zahlte I/1
pay back (to) zurückzahlen I/2
perfect perfekt I/4
petrol station Tankstelle I/2
phobia Phobie I/3
pick (to) pflücken I/4
plan (to) vorhaben I/2
plans Pläne I/2
playroom Spielzimmer I/3
pleasure Freude I/1
pointed spitzig I/4
prayer Gebet I/4
prison Gefängnis I/1
protect (to) schützen I/3
public property
öffentliches Eigentum I/4
purse Geldbeutel I/2
put (to) stellen I/3
realise (to)
begreifen / erkennen I/1
relaxed entspannt I/2
relief Erleichterung I/3
remind (to)
jdn. an etwas erinnern I/4
retire (to)
in den Ruhestand treten I/4
rhododendrons
Rhododendren I/4
ribbon (Haar-) Schleife I/4
road Straße I/3
ruler Lineal I/4
satisfied zufrieden I/3
scold (to) beschimpfen I/4
scratch Kratzer I/3
sedative Beruhigungsmittel I/3
send / **sent** (to)
schicken / schickte I/4
settle down (to) ich einleben I/3
shadow Schatten I/2
shares Aktien I/2
sharp scharf I/2
silence Stille I/3
silent (hier) totenstill I/4
smack (to)
einen Klaps *geben* I/4
solution Lösung I/1
sports car Sportwagen I/2
stiff steif I/3
stone Stein I/3
straight (hier) glatt I/4

street gang Straßenbande I/2
studies Studium I/2
successful erfolgreich I/2
survive (to) überleben I/2
suspiciously mißtrauisch I/2
Switzerland Schweiz I/2
tail Schwanz I/3
take off (to) (hier) Kleider ausziehen I/2
teach / **taught** (to) unterrichten / unterrichtete I/2
tears Tränen I/1
terrified (to be) erschrocken sein I/4
terrorist Terrorist I/1
thief / **thieves** Dieb I/4
tight (hier) fest I/4
top Gipfel I/3
topic Thema I/1
translate (to) übersetzen I/2
tremble (to) zittern I/2
uncomfortable beklommen I/2
unconscious bewußtlos I/3
valuable wertvoll I/2
vet Tierarzt I/3
vomit (to) sich übergeben I/2
wag (to) wedeln I/3
walk past (to) vorbeigehen I/2
water bowl Wassernapf I/3
wave (to) winken I/2
weave / **wove** (to) weben / webte I/4
wire-haired rauhaarig I/3
wood (hier) Waldung I/4
wreath Kranz I/1
yawn (to) gähnen I/2

Notizen